HOW TO DRAW CUTE STUFF

Catherine V. Holmes

Dedicated to Charlotte and Taya.

A big thank you to all the cool kids at
Vinal School for their "cute" ideas.

WELCOME TO "HOW TO DRAW CUTE STUFF"

This cool book is made especially for young artists, their parents, and art teachers who want to find the simplest and most effective ways to learn (and teach!) the art of drawing. This book is jam-packed with easy-to-understand lessons, each split into bite-sized steps, using simple lines and shapes to teach the student the basics of how to draw cute stuff in a way that's easy to understand and simple to implement.

We're also going to dive into the vibrant world of Kawaii. Kawaii drawings are all about happy characters with big eyes and simple shapes, they often have fun proportions, like heads that are bigger than their bodies, making them look cute and young. This book not only teaches the principles of Kawaii, but also gives the artist tools and references for future use.

Lastly, to help your budding artist, I've also sprinkled helpful hints throughout each lesson to make understanding each drawing concept easier. And the best part? After you finish a drawing, you get to color it however you like!

So, it's time to get our pencils ready and start drawing!

HOW TO USE THIS BOOK

1. SIT UPRIGHT!

Sitting upright at a desk improves focus, maintains good posture, and helps prevent back pain! Sitting is great but standing at an easel is great, too!

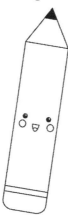

2.USE A PENCIL

Every great artist starts with a pencil; it's where creativity meets possibility. Pencil allows an artist to plan where the parts of their work will be placed. Light pencil lines are also easier to erase if you make a mark you don't like.

3.NO ERASER NEEDED!

No guidelines to erase! Artists often erase and redraw as they create their art. Guidelines are usually used to help size everything up. Sometimes the guidelines get erased, and sometimes they just get covered up. Not here! Just a few simple steps with all the lines you need!

# HOW TO USE THIS BOOK

4. DRAW LIGHTLY

Make sure to draw lightly at first. If you do make a mark that you do not like, it will be much easier to erase if you want to.

5. DON'T TRY TO BE PERFECT!

It's okay if everything isn't just right - pobody's nerfect! Just do your best, follow the steps, and most importantly, enjoy the fun of drawing!

6. JUST HAVE FUN!

Drawing is all about having FUN! You don't need to follow the steps perfectly - the real goal is to enjoy doodling and let your imagination fly!

HOW TO DRAW CUTE STUFF!

7. OUTLINE!

Use a fine pen to draw over your pencil lines
so they look darker and really stand out.

8. COLOR

Pastel colors, bright colors and soft colors
work best, but it is up to you to decide what
colors to use. Add a light pink cheeky blush
tone under the eyes - your drawing will look
even cuter!

WHAT IS "CUTE"?

Characteristics of a "cute" drawing that has a face:

1. Large round heads
2. Eyes spaced wide apart
3. Eyes, nose, and mouth close together
4. Oversized ears (if any)
5. Body smaller than the head

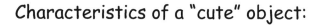

Characteristics of a "cute" object:

1. Make everything round - no pointy edges
2. Pastel and light rainbow colors, no shading needed
3. Black outlines
4. Simplified parts

LET'S DRAW SOME CUTE STUFF

CUTE ALIEN

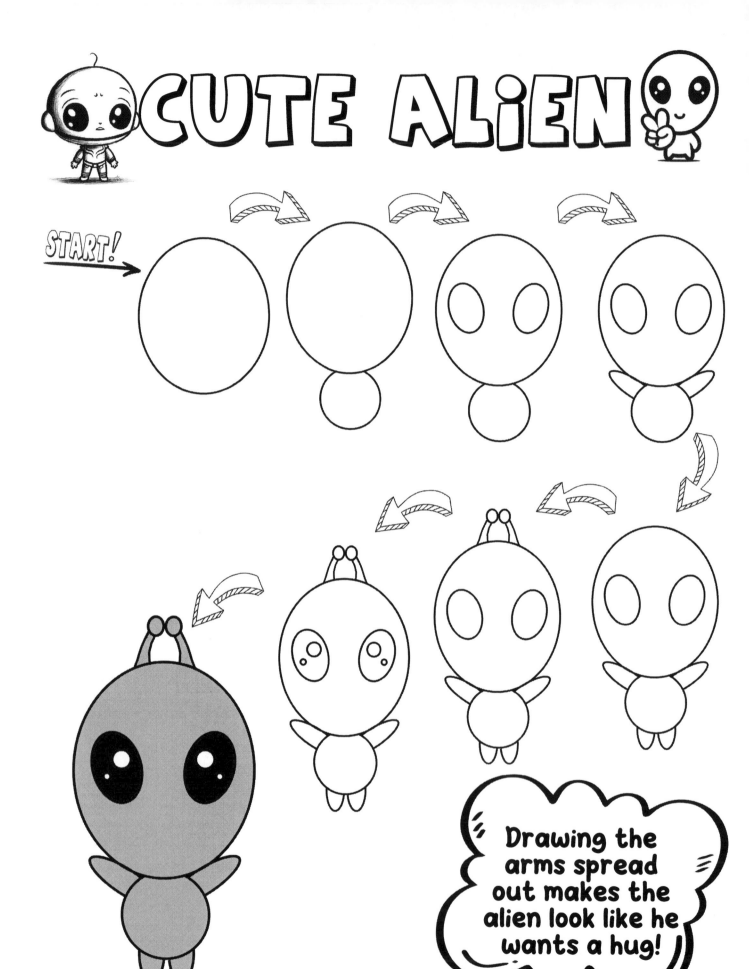

START!

Drawing the arms spread out makes the alien look like he wants a hug!

10

ANGLER FiSH

START!

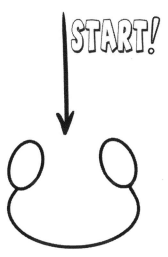

Check out the zig-zag lines at the top of the head.

Draw triangle or curved teeth of varying sizes.

Make some curved lines around the light at the top to look like it is glowing. Color or shade as desired!

11

APPLE

START!

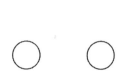

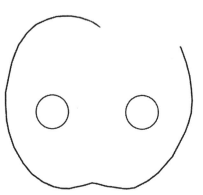

The open mouth and wide eyes show excitement!

AVOCADO

START!

Eyes drawn with simple curves look full of joy and laughter!

13

AXOLOTL

START!

With the arms and legs at random positions, this little guy looks like he is floating!

Draw a wavy line around the tail and dots around the gills for detail!

BABY

START!

The head here is much larger in proportion to the body. The larger-than-normal head makes the cartoon figure seem cuter and more childlike.

BABY PENGUIN

START!

The bigger the eyes (and the shiny spots in them), the cuter the critter!

16

BANANA

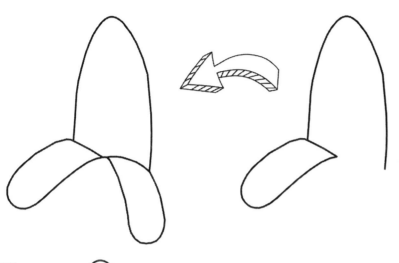

START!

Think of the peels as long letter "U's"

 # BEAR LOLLI

START!

Draw a simple spiral inside of the lollipop for the candy swirl

18

BIRDY

START!

The tiny beak and large eyes help this bird to appear super cute and baby-like.

19

BOBA

START!

The winking eye is simply a sideways triangle shape.

When you wink at someone, you look toward them and close one eye very briefly, usually as a signal that something is a joke or a secret.

20

BUNNY

 START!

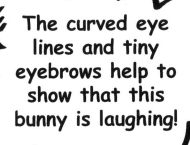

The curved eye lines and tiny eyebrows help to show that this bunny is laughing!

21

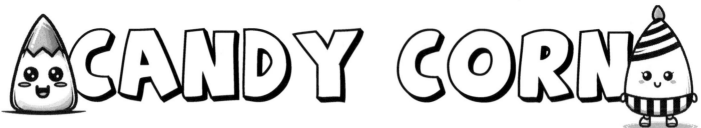

CANDY CORN

START!

Instead of making a triangle with pointy corners, try rounding the edges.

CAPYBARA

START!

The short legs and round body make the capybara extra cute!

CRITTER

START!

This little critter is just as cute from the side view.

CASTLE

Start with a square and build it from there!

START!

CAT BURGER

START!

The small, widely spaced eyes and tiny mouth create a cute and innocent look.

CEREAL

Leave a small opening in your oval to leave space for the spoon.

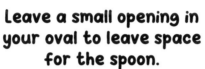

Draw circles inside of circles in the bowl for cereal . . or draw your own shapes!

27

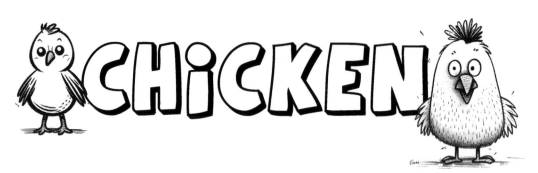

CHICKEN

START!

Use a scalloped line to make the ruffle under the chicken's head.

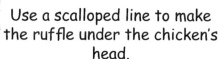

Scalloped objects are decorated with a series of small curves along the edges.

28

COMPUTER

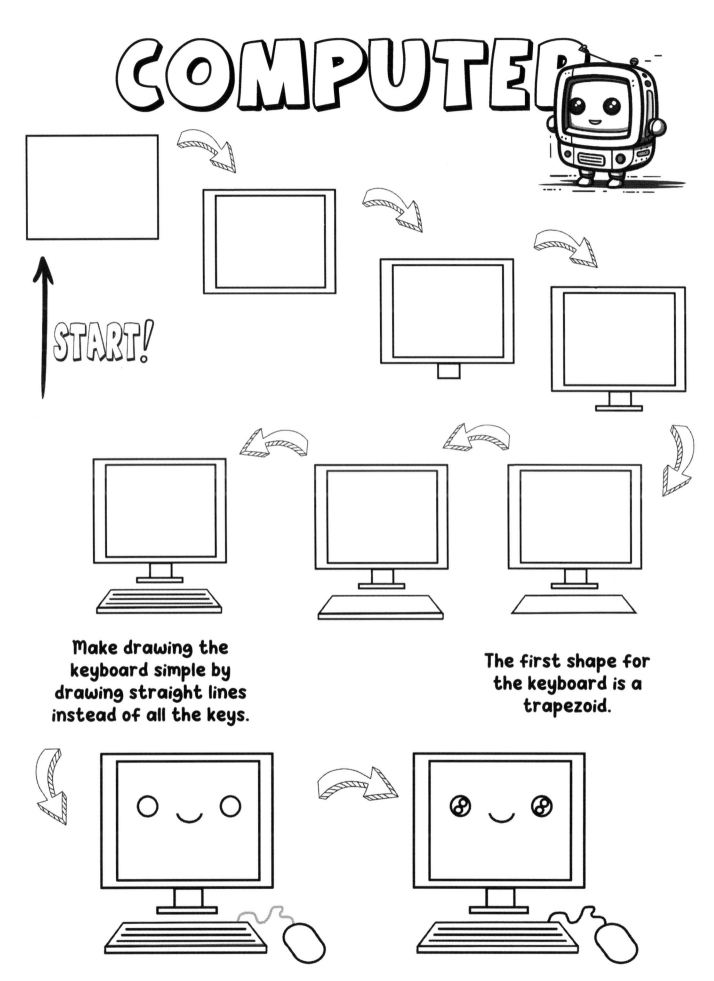

START!

Make drawing the keyboard simple by drawing straight lines instead of all the keys.

The first shape for the keyboard is a trapezoid.

COOKIE

START!

Vary the shape of your scalloped line by drawing some curves small and others large. It will look like a real bite mark!

Try doing an uneven scalloped line on the edge of the circle to show a bite has been taken out of the cookie.

Draw shapes on the cookie for texture

30

CORGi

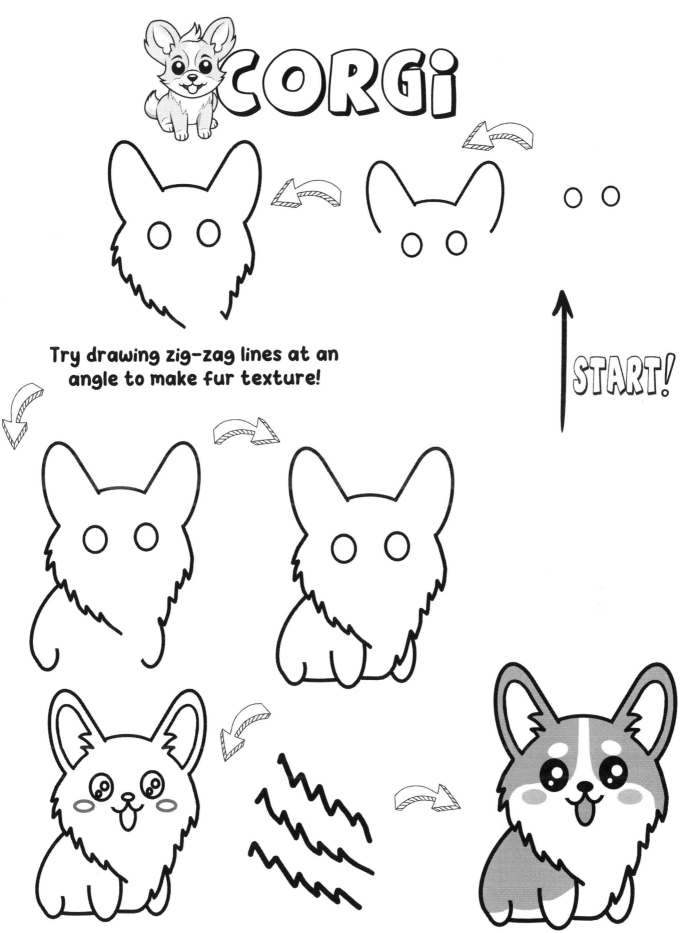

Try drawing zig-zag lines at an angle to make fur texture!

START!

Don't forget to draw little zig-zag lines inside the ears!

COTTON CANDY

START!

Curve the lines on the cone so that it looks "3D"

The cone is a super skinny triangle.

The cotton candy is simply a bunch of curves rounded into a cloud shape

START!

COW

A simple circle is a great start to this cute cow's head.

CUPCAKE

Start with a scalloped line

START!

Think of the sides of the frosting as a cloud. Practice drawing attached curved lines.

The stripes on the base wrapper are wider at the top, leaner at the bottom.

DiNO

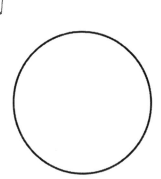

START!

The foot position shows that the Dino is sitting down.

 # DONUT

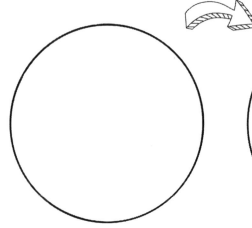

 START!

 Circles can be tough to draw free hand. Find a cup or other round object and trace it to make drawing easier!

FiSH

Draw a crescent moon shape inside each bubble for a shiny spot.

FLOPPY BUNNY

START!

Start with a large oval shape for the head. Leave a space on both sides for the ears.

Add a single line next to each eye for a simple eyelash

FLUFFY SHEEP

Start with a scalloped line drawn around an imaginary circle. This is the perfect cloud-shaped body for your cute sheep.

START!

START! FOX

The curved eye line and tiny smile help to make this fox look like he is resting peacefully.

40

FRIED EGG

A circle, wavy lines and a face is all you need to create this cute fried egg!

START!

Add crescent shape in the yolk to show its roundness.

FROG

START! →

Adding "extra's" to your drawing like this lily-pad and grass, give your character a setting and help to make your art even cuter!

GHOST

START!

The tiny circle mouth and
raised eyebrows show
surprise.

Use a wavy line at
the bottom

GiNGERBREAD

START!

Decorate your gingerbread with circles, swirls and shapes that look like candies.

HAMSTER

START!

Big shiny eyes make the critter look innocent!

HAPPY TIGER

Start with an oval head

START!

Don't forget the little lines for claws!

Simple triangles make a great stripe pattern!

46

HARD CANDY

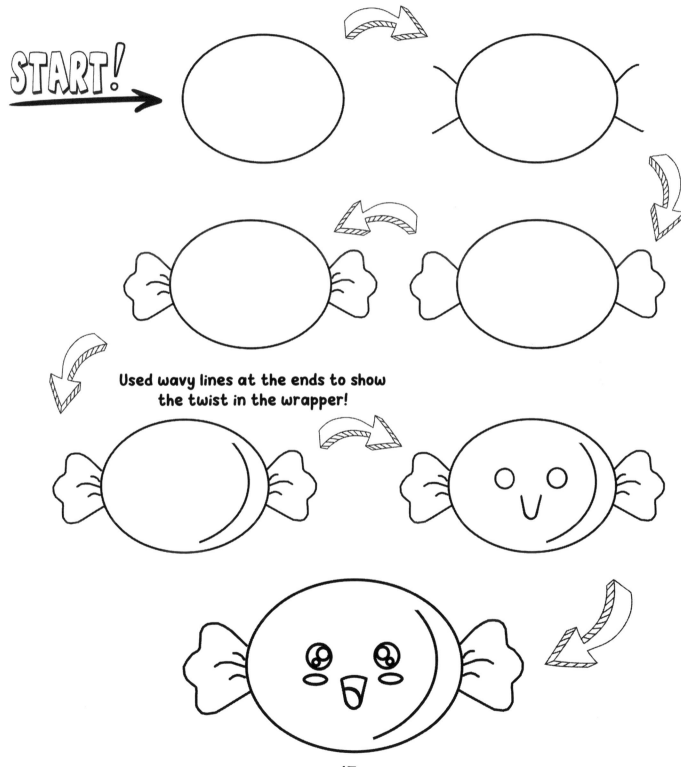

START!

Used wavy lines at the ends to show the twist in the wrapper!

ICE CREAM

START!

The criss-cross lines
make the cone look more
detailed!

MORE iCE CREAM!

Stack ovals on top of one another with a curve on top for the soft serve style.

START!

 # JELLY FiSH

START!

Start with a 1/2 circle

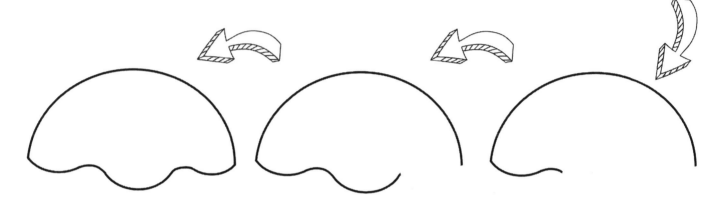

Draw long, squiggly
lines under the jelly for
tentacles.

The simple curved mouth line
makes the jelly look happy.

50

START! KITTY

The large head, chubby body, and round eyes make this kitty look super-cute!

Don't forget to add the tiny toe lines and short whiskers!

51

KiTTY ON BACK

START! →

Drawing from different perspectives can make your art more fun! Try drawing this kitty on its back. This way we can get a peek at those cute little paws!

LION

START! →

A zigzag line is drawn with a lot of short, sharp turns that move up and down. The letter "Z" is a zigzag!

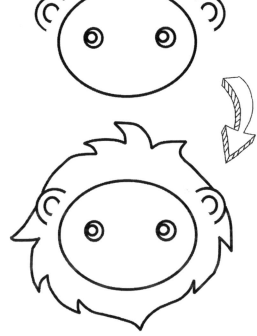

The zig-zag lines drawn around the circle head make a very cute mane!

Draw a simple upside down triangle for the nose.

53

LLAMA

START!

Don't forget to make long straight lines for the neck!

The circle cheeks and 1/2 circle closed eyes make a cheerful face!

START!

MILK

This milk carton is based on a simple 3D cube.

START! MONKEY

Add bump for cheek!

Have your monkey holding something to create even more interest and cuteness.

MOUSE

START!

The hands touching, closed eyes and happy mouth show excitement!

MUSHROOM HOUSE

Make your house look 3D by showing a bit of the underside of the mushroom cap. 3D shapes are measured by length, width, and depth. They don't appear flat, like 2D shapes.

START!

Add curves to the sides to make them round.

PANDA

START!

Start with one flat line on the bottom and work your way up from there to build this cute panda!

PENCIL

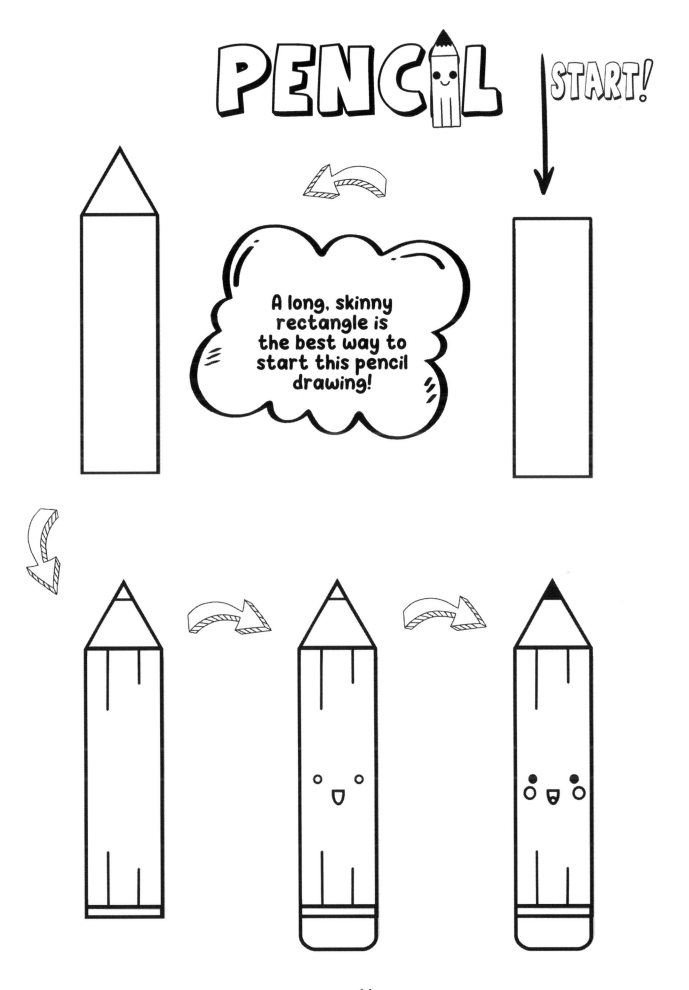

START!

A long, skinny rectangle is the best way to start this pencil drawing!

PIGGY

START! →

Start with a lop-sided circle for the head and nose.

Practice drawing curly lines for the tail and hair.

PiZZA

START! →

The curves under the eyes make the cheeks appear rounded and full.

Draw the tongue sticking out to show it is super tasty!

DON'T FORGET THE TOPPINGS!

Check out some other toppings you can add . . .

PONY

START!

Using curved lines instead of straight and sharp edges, your pony will look plump and dainty.

65

 # POPCORN

 START! →

The curved lines around the outside of the corn help to show motion.

POPCORN BOX

START!

Create the popcorn shape by drawing small half-circles.

POPSICLE

The popsicle is based on a rectangle shape – just round the edges and curve the top!

START!

PUMPKIN

START!

Draw the eyes very close to the mouth. The closer they are together, the more adorable your character will look.

PUPPY

START!

By keeping your drawing simple, you can express a lot with very little. A cute character may not have all of the details (this puppy doesn't even have a nose), but they ooze personality!

START! SAD TOMATO

The simple tear lines (combined with your cute colors) will make this tomato's expression adorable . . .

even though it is sad.

SIMPLE PUP

START!

When you are done drawing,
color or shade a fun pattern
on your pup!

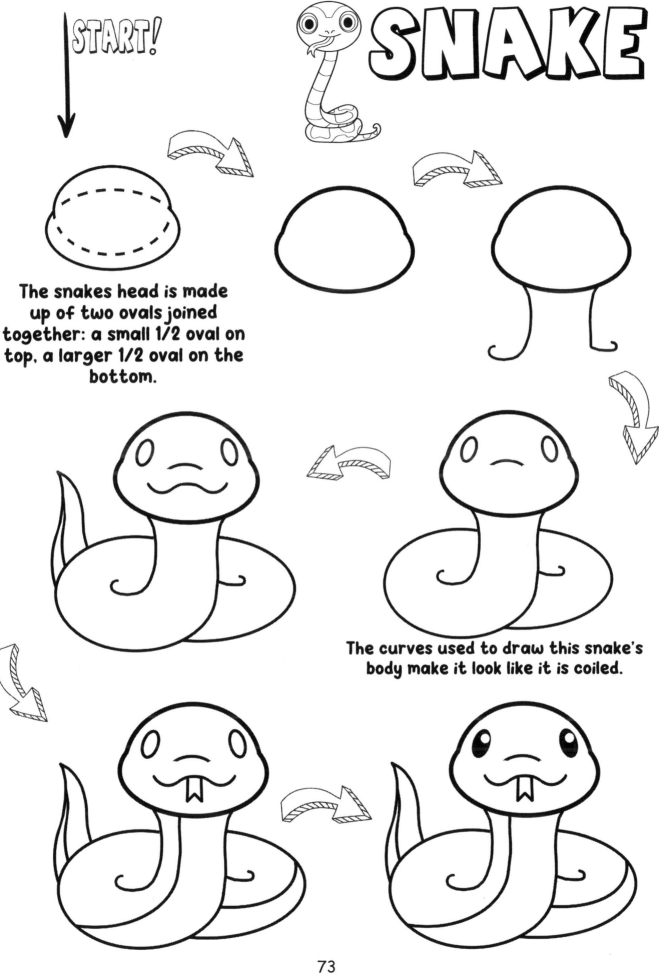

START!

SNAKE

The snakes head is made up of two ovals joined together: a small 1/2 oval on top, a larger 1/2 oval on the bottom.

The curves used to draw this snake's body make it look like it is coiled.

TEACUP

Start with a simple oval for the cup.

Add another oval inside the first for the tea

Little extras like the tea bag add more interest to your artwork. Curved lines on the tea surface show motion

TEA

START!

TEAPOT

This swirly line coming from the spout looks like steam. Practice drawing different swirly, curving lines to add to your drawing.

SEA TURTLE

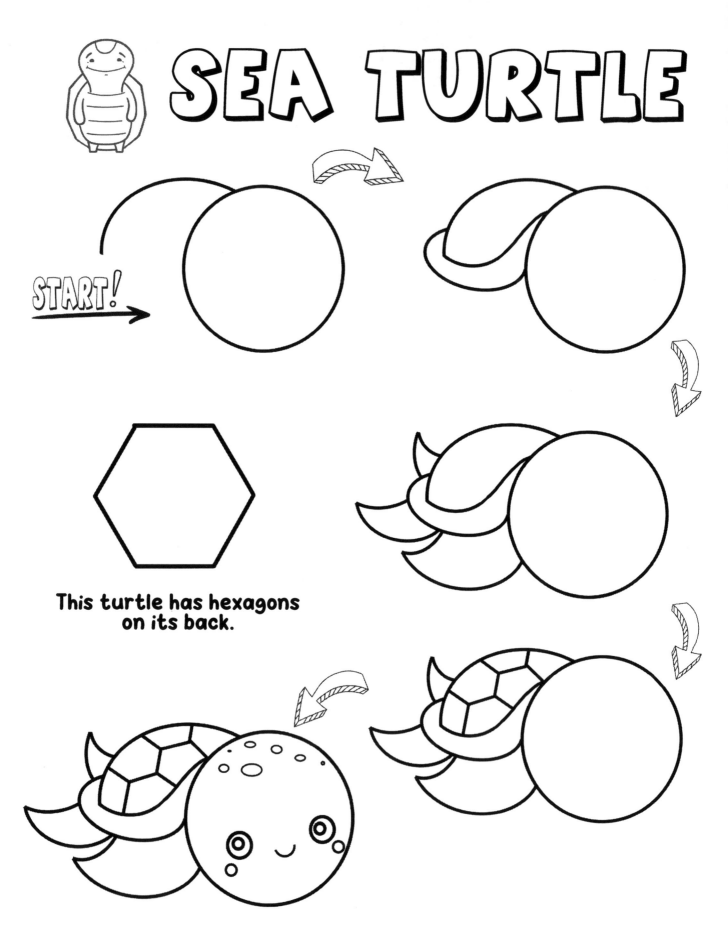

This turtle has hexagons on its back.

Geometric shapes are made of precise points and lines. They include squares, rectangles, triangles, and hexagons.

WATERMELON

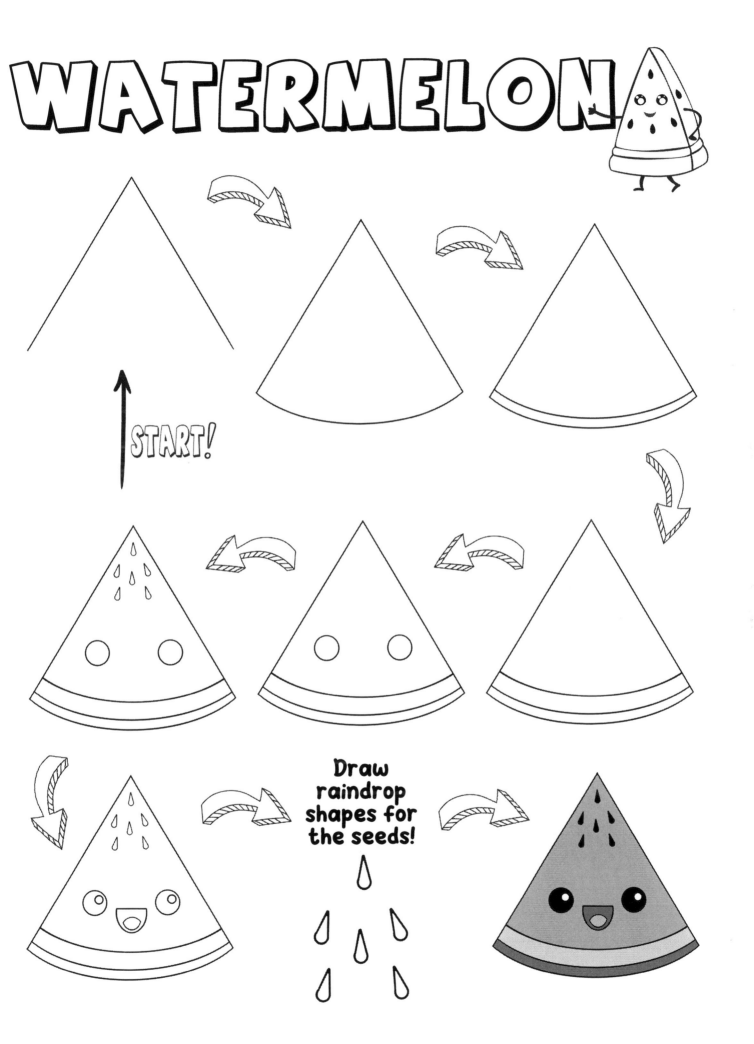

START!

Draw raindrop shapes for the seeds!

WHALE

The body starts with an open circular, curve.

Add a tiny fin

Draw upside down rain drop shapes at the top!

DRAW YOUR OWN!

Ready to try drawing your very own, unique cute character? You can draw any item using the cute style outlined in this book. Here are some ideas for you to use as you build your critter!

Start with a pencil:
Using a pencil first helps you to make quick, sketchy lines that are easy to erase if you don't like the mark you have made.

Make sure to keep it simple:
Drawings should be small and simple. They may even look a little bit squished! Leave out the small details such as fingers and toes.

Cute is small:
You can take any object and make it cute. Draw your item small, make it chubby and round those edges. There are not many pointy edges in a cute drawing.

Add a face:
Smiling, happy faces on objects can make them look cute. Even a sad or angry face can be used on an adorable character. Keep the eyes big, the mouth tiny and you don't even need to add a nose. The face will make your drawing come alive!

Outline:
Use a fine pen or marker to draw over your pencil lines so they look darker and really stand out. Waterproof markers are best since they won't smudge if you want to add color.

Color:
Pastel colors, bright colors and soft colors work best, but it is up to you to decide what colors to use. Add a light pink cheeky blush tone under the eyes - your drawing will look even cuter!

Extra's
Don't forget to add lots of "extra's" to give your artwork a personal touch. This can include whiskers, spots, stripes, hair, accessories and patterns.

Don't be afraid to experiment and have fun!

FACIAL FEATURES

Eyes

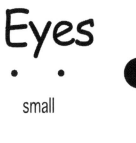

small

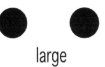

large

winking

squinting

joyful

sleepy

mad

bored

shiny

"x" eyes

pretty

sad

oval

cheerful

tears

love

Mouths

happy

silly

sad

surprised

toothy grin

mad

animal

frustrated

sick

tasty

open

MORE FACE IDEAS

Cheeks

round   oval   blush lines   blush lines in circle

Noses & Muzzles

tiny   half oval   snout   rounded triangle   small oval

cheeky   triangle   combo   circle   simple curve

Ears

half oval   double round   rounded triangle

big ovals   short points   long points

 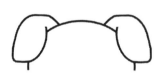 

long floppy   short floppy   top ovals

Practice Drawing Faces!

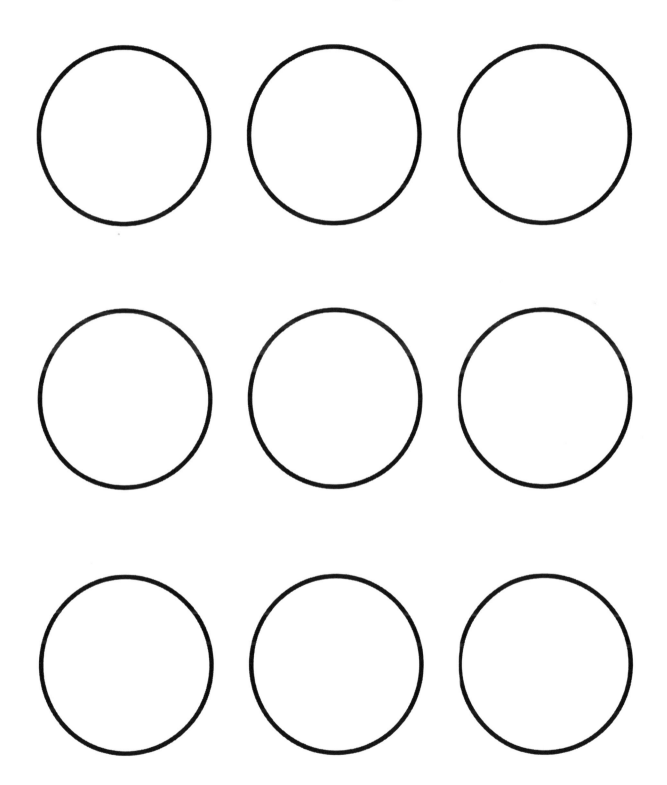

KAWAII ART

These cute, tiny and lovable drawings are inspired by Japanese kawaii art. There is a whole cuteness-culture of kawaii in Japan that spans beyond drawing and includes fashion, colorful cafes, anime characters, cute hand writing styles, animal mascots, make up and a variety of commercial products.

The kawaii art style is drawn with simple black outlines, round edges and few details. Kawaii subject matter includes humans and animals that are charming, shy and childlike. These drawings are often made with big heads, large eyes spread wide apart and little bodies in order to look like babies. Sometimes, faces are put on everyday objects like gadgets, sweet treats and even furniture to make them come alive! They are colored with bright or pastel colors and are always adorable.

KAWAII FOOD

KAWAii CATS

KAWAii CRiTTERS

MORE CRITTERS

KAWAII FACES

iNSPiRATiONS!
Draw Your Own Cute Stuff

How to Draw Cool Stuff
Other Books in the Series

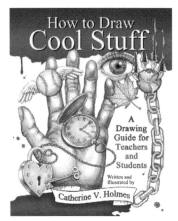

How to Draw Cool Stuff: A Drawing Guide for Teachers and Students
This book shows simple step-by-step illustrations that make it easy for anyone to draw cool stuff with precision and confidence. These lessons will help you see line, shape, space and other elements in everyday objects and turn them into detailed works of art in just a few simple steps. The exercises in this book will help train your brain so you can visualize ordinary objects in a different manner, allowing you to see through the eyes of an artist. From photorealistic faces to holiday themes and tattoo drawings, How to Draw Cool Stuff makes drawing easier than you would think and more fun than you ever imagined!

How to Draw Cool Stuff: Basics, Shading, Texture, Pattern and Optical Illusions is the second book in the *How to Draw Cool Stuff* series. Inside you will find simple illustrations that cover the necessities of drawing cool stuff. Specific exercises are provided that offer step-by-step guidelines for drawing a variety of subjects. Each lesson starts with an easy-to-draw shape that will become the basic structure of the drawing. From there, each step adds elements to that structure, allowing the artist to build on their creation and make a more detailed image. Starting with the basic forms, the artist is provided a guide to help see objects in terms of simplified shapes. Instructions for shading to add depth, contrast, character and movement to a drawing are then covered.

How to Draw Cool Stuff: Holidays, Seasons and Events is a step-by-step drawing guide that illustrates popular celebrations, holidays and events for your drawing pleasure. From the Chinese New Year to April Fools' Day, Father's Day to Halloween, Christmas and New Year's Eve - this book covers over 100 fun days, holidays, seasons and events, and offers simple lessons that will teach you how to draw like a pro and get you in the spirit of whichever season it may be! The third book in the How To Draw Cool Stuff series, this exciting new title will teach you how to create simple illustrations using basic shapes and a drawing technique that simplifies the process of drawing, all while helping you construct height, width and depth in your work. It will guide you through the creative thought process and provide plenty of ideas to get you started. The lessons in this book will also teach you how to think like an artist and remind you that you are only limited by your imagination!

How to Draw Cool Stuff
Other Books in the Series

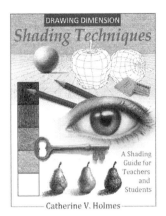

Shading is one of the easiest ways of adding depth, contrast, character, and movement to your drawings. By controlling pencil pressure and stroke, understanding light and having knowledge of blending techniques, an artist can enhance their work and offer the "wow" factor needed to produce realistic artworks. **Drawing Dimension - A Shading Guide for Teachers and Students** offers a series of shading tutorials that are easy to understand and simple to follow. It goes beyond the standard "step by step" instruction to offer readers an in-depth look at a variety of shading techniques and their applications. The book is perfectly suitable for beginners and moderates of all ages, students and teachers, professionals and novices; anyone can learn how to shade like a pro!

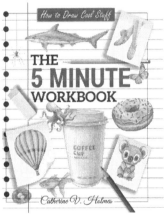

Five minutes may not seem like a lot of time to allow yourself to work on a drawing, as artists have been known to take days, months, and even years to complete a single work of art. However, as this book will prove, you can draw some really cool stuff in just under five minutes. By limiting their time, artists will start to see only the most essential parts of a subject while communicating action, movement, and expression into one timed drawing. This book is jam-packed with step-by-step lessons for drawing cool objects quickly – in 5-minutes or less! **How to Draw Cool Stuff: The 5 Minute Workbook** will teach you how to create simple illustrations using basic shapes and a drawing technique that simplifies the process of drawing, all while helping you construct height, width, and depth in your work. It will guide you through the creative thought process and provide plenty of ideas to get you started.

This book was designed for those who dare to explore the darker and more unconventional side of drawing. Within these pages, you'll learn how to create creepy and scary images that are sure to give your friends and family nightmares, and the best part? All of the lessons in this book have been student-tested and teacher approved. That means you can trust that each project is engaging and effective for students of all ages. **How to Draw Awesome Stuff** is jam-packed with interesting and informative drawing lessons that offer clear objectives and foster achievement. Whether you are new to the world of drawing or an intermediate artist, this book will provide you with the necessary tools and inspiration to unleash your creativity and inspire your creative spirit. With easy-to-follow tutorials, you'll learn how to recognize the basic shapes within objects, and how to use these shapes to create images that are both dynamic and visually stunning.

Printed in Poland
by Amazon Fulfillment
Poland Sp. z o.o., Wrocław

25191810R00054